Molecules Are Everywhere!

D1708210

This course was written by
Naturally Curious Expert
Valerie Grosso

Valerie is a microbiologist who is curious about all the microscopic things that make up our world.

Printed by CreateSpace

ISBN 978-1-942403-07-4

www.benaturallycurious.com

Many activities in this book make use of printed materials. If you prefer not to cut them directly from this book, please visit the URL listed below and enter the code for a supplemental PDF containing all printable materials.

URL: www.benaturallycurious.com/molecules-printables/

password: **bond**

Table of Contents

Required materials: Printer and paper, scissors, tape, calcium carbonate chalk (see Let's Experiment! for brand suggestion), white vinegar, string or yarn, Popsicle sticks, eggshells, small bowl or cup

Ellie the Electron Finds a Friend

This is the story of an **ELECTRON** named Ellie. MEET ELLIE. She is a particle that is VERY, VERY small—so small that we can't see her, even with a microscope. Today, we will take an imaginary dive down into Ellie's very small world to help us understand what she does.

First, let's take a look around us. What do you see? You see THINGS. Maybe a chair, maybe a spoon, maybe a window. All the things you see are made of different materials. But what makes your wooden chair different from your metal spoon and different from the glass window? All these things are different because of what they are made of. And to understand what they are made of, down into Ellie's world we must go.

As we've said, Ellie is a particle (a VERY small thing). Ellie, like all other electrons, spends her days circling round and round a center, called a **NUCLEUS**—sort of like how Earth circles around the sun. Together, the nucleus and all the electrons that circle around it are called an **ATOM**.

Can you point out Ellie in the picture? Do you remember what kind of particle she is? That's right, an electron! What is she circling around? You got it! A nucleus. Together, the electrons and nucleus make...what? An atom! Can you pretend to be an electron circling around a nucleus?

Atoms are cool because they are the building blocks used to make everything we see in the world around us! Different kinds of atoms have different numbers of electrons in them. Let's take a look at hydrogen. There are lots of hydrogen atoms in the world, but this one has Ellie's cousin Sam circling around its nucleus. A hydrogen atom has just one electron.

> **A**toms are small particles containing a nucleus and one or more electrons.

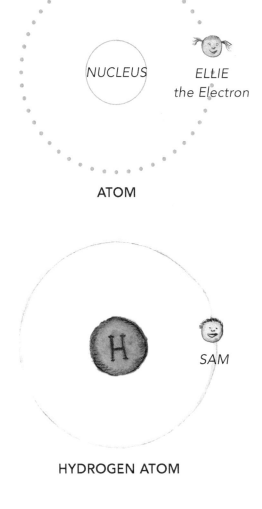

NUCLEUS   ELLIE the Electron

ATOM

SAM

HYDROGEN ATOM

Now let's look at the atom ELLIE is a part of—oxygen. Wow! Oxygen has so many more parts! It has eight electrons circling around it!

Our world is made up of many different types of atoms. You can see all the types of atoms in a chart called the **PERIODIC TABLE OF ELEMENTS**.

An **ELEMENT** is just a "kind" of atom, like vanilla is a kind of ice cream. We have given each type of atom (element) a nickname in the form of a letter (or sometimes two or three letters). For example, oxygen's nickname is "O" and hydrogen's nickname is "H."

Let's look at some more kinds of atoms and their electrons. Other kinds of atoms have different numbers of electrons. (That's part of what makes them different from each other.)

Which is your favorite atom? How many electrons does it have?

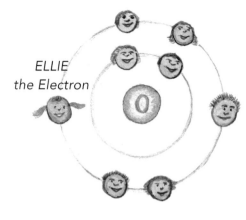

ELLIE
the Electron

OXYGEN

Each different kind of atom is a different element.

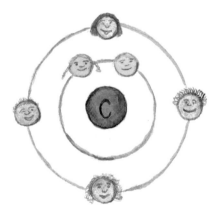

CARBON

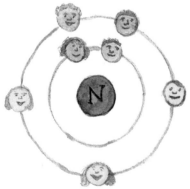

CALCIUM

NITROGEN

What are you
CURIOUS about?

Okay, back to Ellie.

What does she like to do besides circle round and round (which, of course, is very fun!)?

Well, one thing you need to know about electrons is that they are very friendly and don't like to be lonely!

In fact, electrons like to be in pairs! Sometimes in an atom, an electron will already have a friend, but sometimes it will be on its own.

Electrons like to be in pairs!

Let's look at **SAM'S ATOM**. He's all on his own...he doesn't look happy because he *definitely* wants to find a friend.

Now let's look at ELLIE'S ATOM. Some of the electrons in her atom have friends and are happy, but she doesn't, and one other electron in her atom also doesn't.

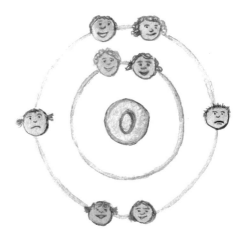

What are you CURIOUS about?

Let's help Ellie find a friend! Now, the first thing you might think of, because you are good at finding friends, is that Ellie could pair up with the other lonely electron in her atom. This, it turns out, is very hard to do...

It is much easier to find an electron friend in a DIFFERENT atom and to pair up THAT way!

Let's see what happens when we put Ellie's atom and Sam's atom near each other. Look! Ellie and Sam are both looking for a friend and have found each other! Fantastic! Now they are happy and will want to stay together! And—look! The other electron in Ellie's atom has also found an electron friend in another hydrogen atom.

WATER MOLECULE (H$_2$0)

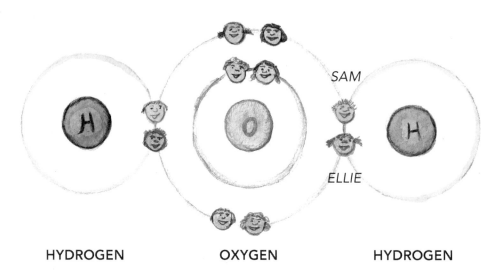

HYDROGEN   OXYGEN   HYDROGEN

Do you know what we have just made? We have made a MOLECULE! When atoms join together, they make MOLECULES.

Different molecules are what make all the things in our world (like the chair, the spoon, and the window) different from each other.

We have actually just made WATER! One oxygen atom and two hydrogen atoms that are joined together by their electrons make a WATER MOLECULE. (In fact, sometimes people call water H$_2$O because there are two hydrogen atoms and one oxygen atom.)

> Different molecules are what make all the things in our world different from each other.

Let's look at a different kind of molecule. This time, we see a carbon atom. Carbon has six electrons, and four of them don't have friends! Let's see if we can find friends for these electrons. Which atoms might you use?

CARBON

Oh, look! Here are four hydrogen atoms—and each one wants to find a friend. Let's match our four lonely carbon electrons with the four lonely hydrogen electrons.

Go ahead and draw lines to pair up the lonely electrons.

Now we have a molecule that has one carbon atom and four hydrogen atoms.

This is a molecule that is common in the world around us (and is a little bit STINKY!). It is called methane.

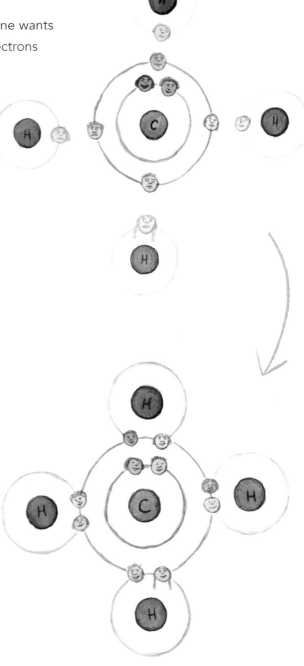

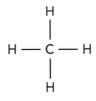

H
|
H — C — H
|
H

METHANE (CH$_4$)

When electrons pair up and bring their atoms together, we call this a **COVALENT BOND**. The bonds between atoms hold molecules together. We draw a bond as a dash between the two letters.

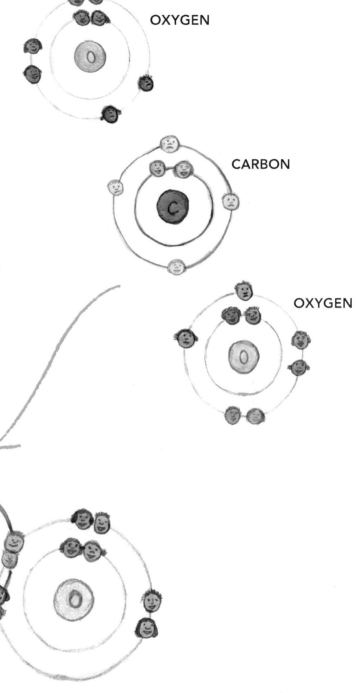

But wait...there is another carbon atom. It can't find four hydrogen atoms, but it does find two oxygen atoms. Do you remember how many lonely electrons EACH oxygen atom has?

That's right, two! Let's see if those two oxygen atoms can make the electrons on the carbon atom happy. They can!

Go ahead and draw lines to connect the lonely electrons!

This molecule—one carbon atom and two oxygen atoms—is called carbon dioxide. Carbon dioxide is what we breathe out when we exhale.

We are so happy that Ellie and Sam found each other and are no longer lonely. Now let's go make our own molecules!!

OXYGEN

CARBON

OXYGEN

CARBON DIOXIDE (CO$_2$)

What are you
CURIOUS about?

Let's Make Molecules!

INSTRUCTIONS

Let's pair up lonely electrons and make our own molecules! Cut out the atoms from pages 25–31 and use the parent guide below to make some molecules. Remember, a line connecting atoms means that two electrons have paired up! Don't worry if your electrons are not facing each other—as long as they are lonely, they can pair up with an electron in another atom! Use tape or glue to join your atoms and attach them to a Popsicle stick. Write the name of the molecule you made on the Popsicle stick.

Challenge: Cut out additional atoms. Can you think of other combinations that might work? Remember, electrons in an atom must usually find friends to be happy!

MATERIALS

- scissors
- tape
- printed atoms from pages 25–31
- Popsicle sticks and glue (optional)

PARENT GUIDE

AMMONIA

$$\begin{array}{c} H \\ | \\ N \\ / \quad \backslash \\ H \qquad H \end{array}$$

CARBON DIOXIDE

$$O \diagdown \diagup O \\ \diagdown \diagup \\ C$$

METHANOL

$$H - \overset{\displaystyle H}{\underset{\displaystyle H}{\overset{|}{\underset{|}{C}}}} - O - H$$

ACTIVITY
1

Let's Make Molecules!

PARENT GUIDE (continued)

METHANE

$$H - \underset{\underset{H}{|}}{\overset{\overset{H}{|}}{C}} - H$$

*molecular**
NITROGEN

N ≡ N

*molecular**
OXYGEN

O = O

*molecular**
HYDROGEN

H — H

ACETIC ACID
(vinegar)

$$H - \underset{\underset{H}{|}}{\overset{\overset{H}{|}}{C}} - \underset{\underset{O}{\parallel}}{C} - O - H$$

GLYCINE
(an amino acid)

$$\underset{H}{\overset{H}{}} N - \underset{\underset{H}{|}}{\overset{\overset{H}{|}}{C}} - \underset{\overset{O}{\parallel}}{C} \overset{O}{\underset{O - H}{}}$$

* We call it "molecular" when
  two of the same atom pair up.

Be a Molecule with Your Friends

INSTRUCTIONS

You've made molecules out of paper—now it's time to be a molecule yourself! First, cut out the atoms page 33 to label yourself and your friends. (You can use tape to stick the atom to your shirt, or make the atom into a necklace with string and hang it around your neck.) Next, decide which molecule in the list below you would like to be. You can be one of the atoms; your friends and your stuffed animals can be the others. Use your hands and feet as lonely electrons to pair up with your friends' lonely electrons. To use your feet, use string to tie each foot together with the foot of your friend or stuffed animal.

Remember, different atoms have differing numbers of lonely electrons, so you will need different numbers of partners for different molecules!

When you have made your molecule, can you act out where it is found? If your molecule is found in more than one place, can you act out the different places?

> ### MATERIALS
>
> - four friends or stuffed animals (or a combination of both)
> - scissors
> - printed atoms from page 33
> - tape (or string)

ACTIVITY 2

Be a Molecule with Your Friends

PARENT GUIDE

H — H

molecular
HYDROGEN

This is a gas!

O = O

molecular
OXYGEN

This is a gas and is part of the air around us. We breathe it!

N ≡ N

molecular
NITROGEN

This is a gas in the air around us. Most of the molecules in air are nitrogen.

CARBON DIOXIDE

This is a gas we breathe out. Can you pretend you are being breathed out?

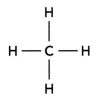

METHANE

This is a gas found in the ground. We can burn it for heat and to cook.

AMMONIA

This is a molecule used to clean the house!

ACTIVITY
3

Electron Match Card Game

INSTRUCTIONS

Let's see who can pair up molecules to get the most points! Electron Match Card Game starts by gently shuffling the cards and dealing five cards to each player (minimum two players). Place the remaining cards face down in the middle. The youngest player starts first and selects a card from the pile. When a player can pair up electrons to make a molecule with no lonely electrons, the player puts those cards down and earns the points shown on the cards. For example, if a player gets a C and two O's, those cards are put down, and seven points are earned. After a player has made a molecule, he or she can replace those cards with cards from the pile. Feel free to spread cards out behind you to make sure you're seeing them all. The game ends when no more molecules can be made. The player with the most points wins!

MATERIALS

- scissors
- print out cards on pages 35–39 (ideally on card stock which is harder to see through)

PARENT GUIDE

H — H

molecular
HYDROGEN

H

|

H — C — H

|

H

METHANE

O = O

molecular
OXYGEN

N ≡ N

molecular
NITROGEN

H

|

N

H   H

AMMONIA

O   O

C

CARBON DIOXIDE

ACTIVITY
4

Let's Experiment! Make New Molecules

We've seen that molecules are all around us. Now let's change some molecules!

When atoms in a molecule let go of each other's electrons, they become free to pair up with other atoms. This means that some molecules will come apart to make new ones. This process is called a **CHEMICAL REACTION**.

During a chemical reaction, atoms in molecules rearrange to form new molecules.

In our experiment today, we will start with two types of molecules: calcium carbonate and vinegar, which can also be called acetic acid. Here's what those two molecules look like. Calcium carbonate is made up of a calcium atom and several other atoms, which, together, are called carbonate. (Calcium and carbonate don't actually share electrons—they are joined by a different kind of bond called an ionic bond.)

CALCIUM CARBONATE

Ca

ACETIC ACID (vinegar)

So what happens when we put these two together? Let's find out!

For calcium carbonate, we are going to use regular white chalk. Start by placing a piece of chalk in a small bowl or cup. Pour vinegar over the chalk so that the vinegar covers the chalk.

What do you observe? Write down your observations in your Experimental Journal on page 17.

Do you see bubbles in the vinegar that weren't there before? This is carbon dioxide, which you remember from your Making Molecules activity. We will see below how the carbon and oxygen from the calcium carbonate are no longer attached to the calcium, so now they are carbon dioxide!

If you leave the chalk in the vinegar for a while, when you come back you will see that the chalk is gone and there is now white powder at the bottom of the bowl. This is calcium acetate. When the calcium let go of the carbon dioxide, it joined up with some of the oxygen and hydrogen atoms from the vinegar to make a different molecule, calcium acetate.

MATERIALS

• calcium carbonate chalk (white blackboard chalk, such as Prang— make sure your chalk is calcium carbonate)

• white vinegar

• eggshells

• small bowl or cup

ACTIVITY
4

Experimental Journal

Record the steps in your experiment (What did you do?):

_____

_____

_____

_____

_____

_____

What did you observe?

_____

_____

_____

_____

_____

What do you think would be interesting to try next? Why?

_____

_____

_____

_____

_____

Let's Experiment! Make New Molecules

ACTIVITY 4

INSTRUCTIONS (continued)

To understand what is going on with the chalk and vinegar, let's look at the drawings of the chemicals below. You see both of our starting molecules: calcium carbonate and two acetic acid molecules. See what happens when we mix the two types of molecules together: All the red atoms from acetic acid now join with calcium to make calcium acetate. The blue oxygen from calcium carbonate joins up with two hydrogen atoms from acetic acid to make water. The yellow carbon and oxygen atoms from calcium carbonate are now left as carbon dioxide!

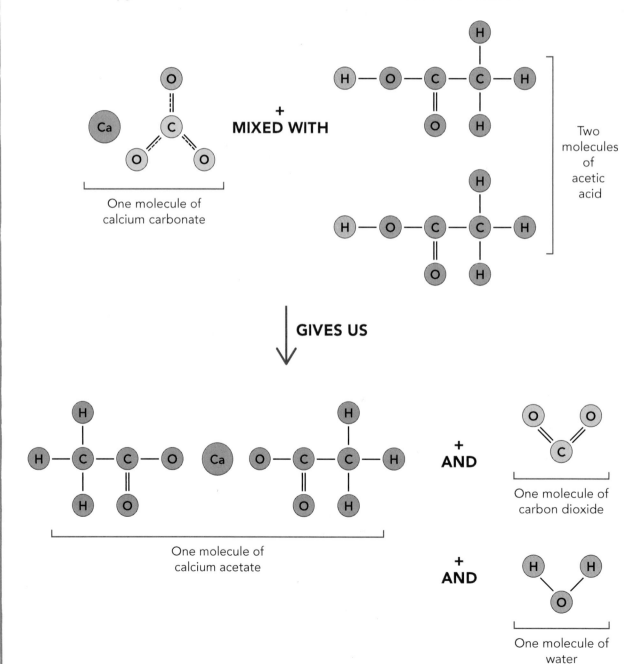

ACTIVITY
4

Let's Experiment! Make New Molecules

INSTRUCTIONS (continued)

Now, look at the molecule diagram on page 41. Cut out the sets of atoms on the left side of the page. See if you can move the sets of atoms around to act out the chemical reaction from the previous page!

Chalk isn't the only thing that is made of calcium carbonate. You can also try taking an eggshell, rinsing it off, and putting it in the vinegar. This time, the molecules might switch their atoms around more slowly so you might not see the carbon dioxide bubbles. But if you leave the eggshell in the vinegar for a day, come back and see how the eggshell feels. Write down your observations on the next page!

What are you CURIOUS about?

Experimental Journal

Record the steps in your experiment (What did you do?):

_____

_____

_____

_____

_____

_____

_____

What did you observe?

_____

_____

_____

_____

_____

What do you think would be interesting to try next? Why?

_____

_____

_____

_____

_____

Curiosity Connector

Here are some links to help you follow your curiosity!

- Make some more molecules using gumdrops and toothpicks:
  http://www.sciencenter.org/climatechange/d/cart_activity_guide_lets_make_
  molecules.pdf

- Make models of your molecules with a kit:
  http://www.amazon.com/FloraCraft-Styrofoam-Molecule-Model-Pre-
  Painted/dp/B00114LXK0/ref=sr_1_10?ie=UTF8&qid=1369850874&sr=8-
  10&keywords=molecule+kit

- A worksheet for building more molecules:
  http://www.parents.com/blogs/homeschool-den/tag/molecules-for-kids/

- A free online game to make molecules:
  http://www.learn4good.com/games/educational-learning-activities/
  chemistrypuzzles.htm

- A video showing how atoms come together to make molecules:
  http://www.sciencekids.co.nz/videos/chemistry/molecules.html

- Ideas from teachers on how to model molecules:
  http://www.proteacher.org/c/457_Atoms_and_Molecules.html

- A molecule-making activity from the Magic School Bus:
  http://www.scholastic.com/magicschoolbus/parentteacher/activities/molly.htm

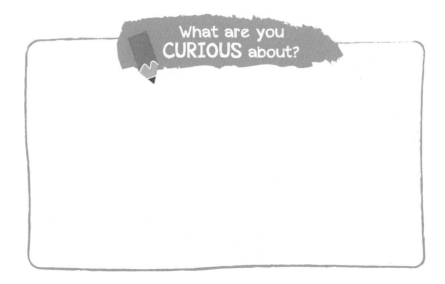

What are you CURIOUS about?

Glossary

ATOMS – Microscopic particles that are the building blocks of molecules. They each contain a nucleus and one or more electrons.

CHEMICAL REACTION – A process in which atoms from different molecules rearrange to form new molecules.

COVALENT BOND – When two lonely electrons from different atoms pair up, they hold the atoms together with a covalent bond and create a molecule.

ELECTRON – Part of an atom that circles around the nucleus.

ELEMENT – A type of atom. Different elements have different numbers of electrons.

MOLECULE – Multiple atoms joined together by bonds. Different molecules have different physical and chemical properties and are what make all the physical things in our world different from each other.

NUCLEUS – The center of an atom.

PERIODIC TABLE OF ELEMENTS – A chart that shows all the different kinds of elements found in our world.

Tools for Your Tool Kit

Let's make the ideas you learned today part of your life tool kit. Remember to print out some blank tool kit pages and tape or glue on today's tools.

1. Molecules are made of different kinds of _____ .

   Add a **MOLECULE** to your tool kit!

2. What circles around an atom? _____

   Put an **ELECTRON** in your tool kit!

3. Would electrons rather be on their own or part of a pair? _____

   Add a **COVALENT BOND** to your tool kit!

4. Can electrons that pair up come apart again? _____

   Add a **CHEMICAL REACTION** to your tool kit!

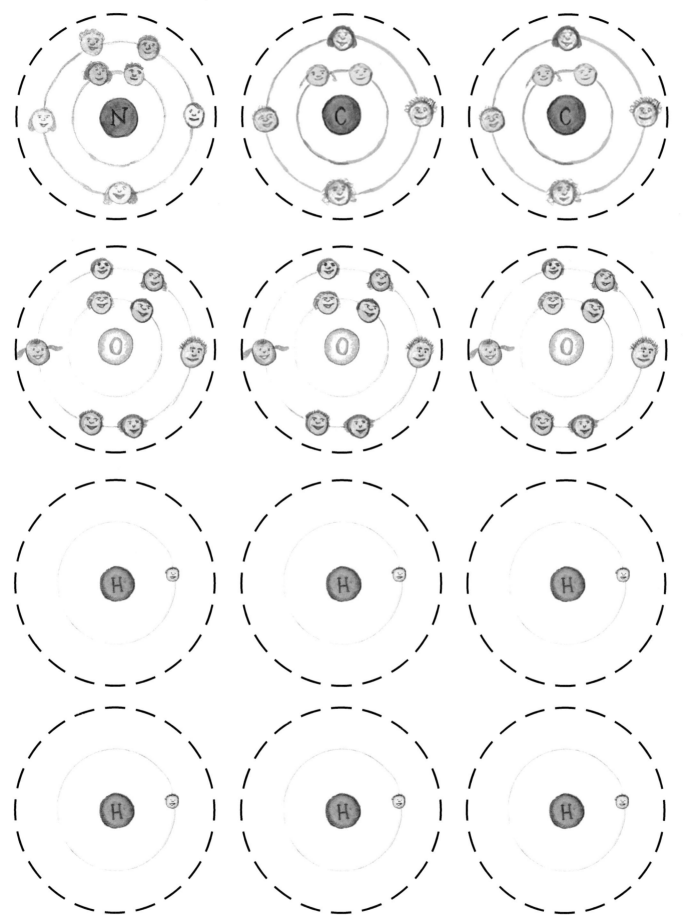

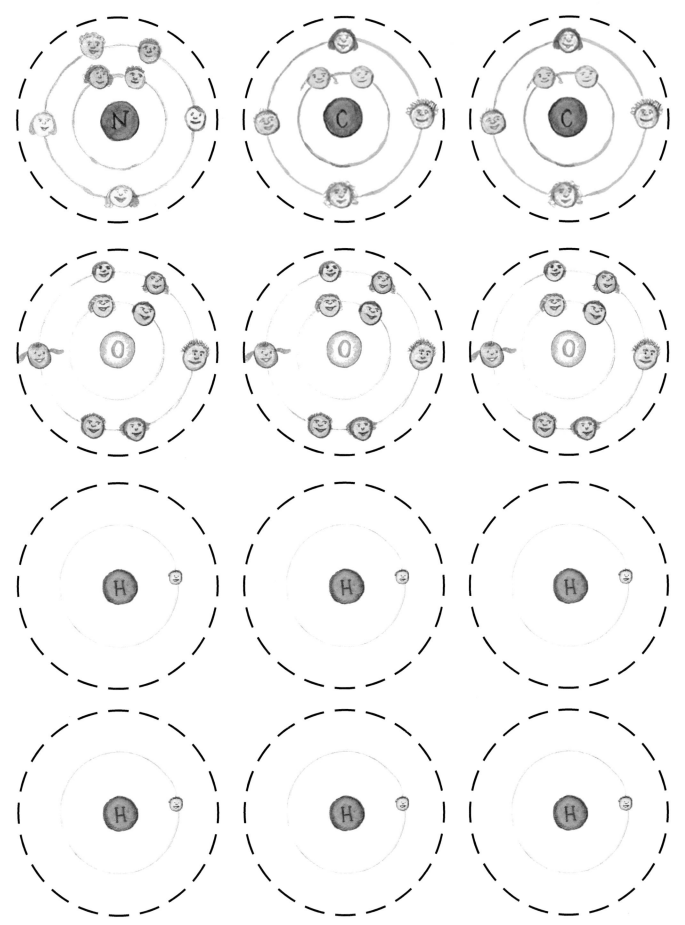

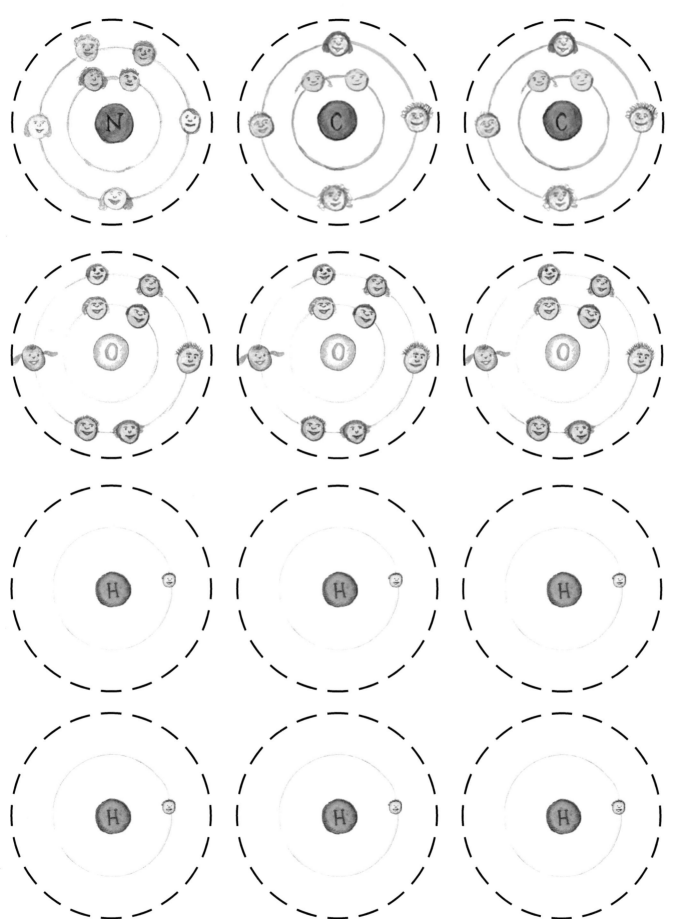

Cutouts for Activity 1: Let's Make Molecules!

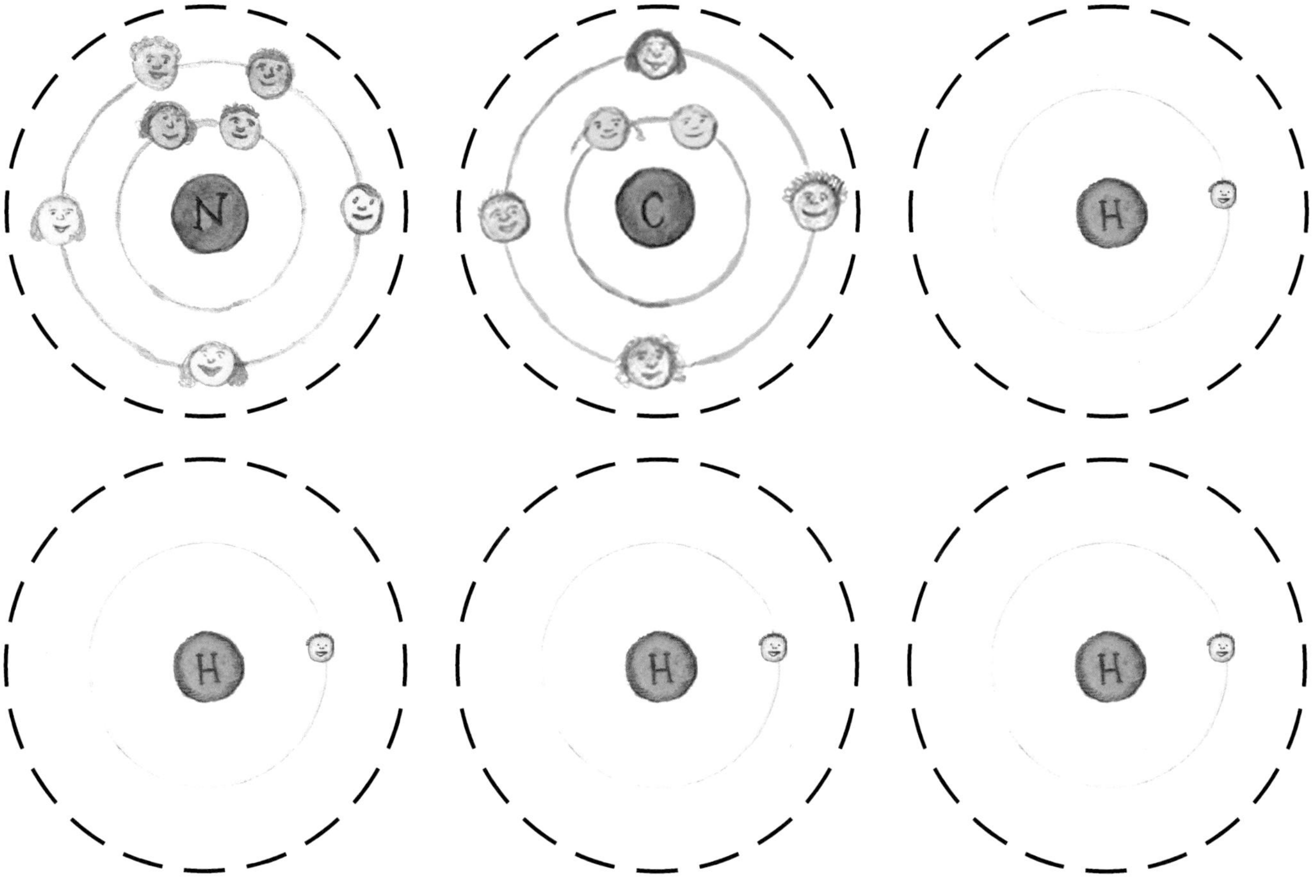

Cutouts for Activity 2: Be a Molecule with Your Friends

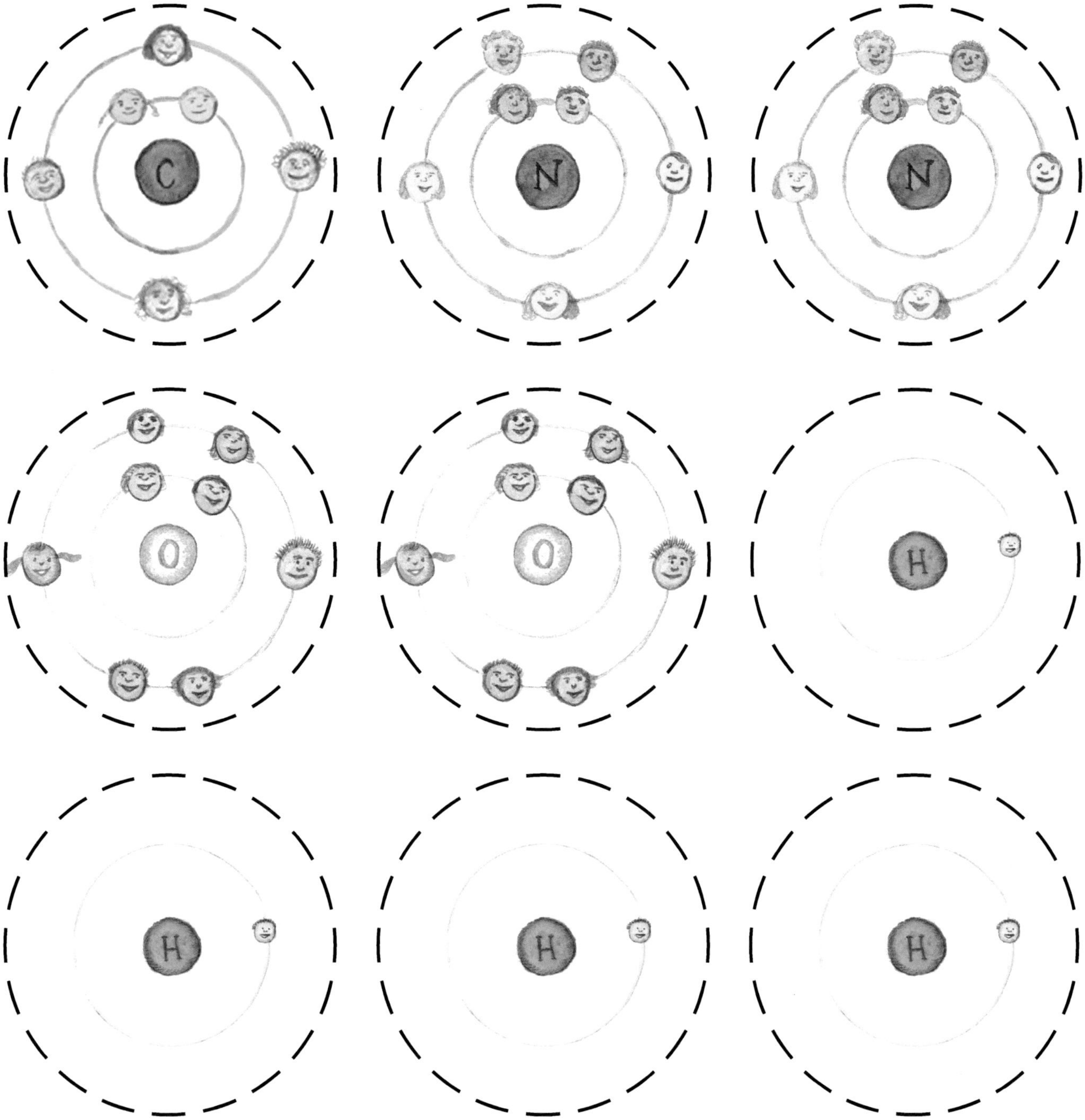

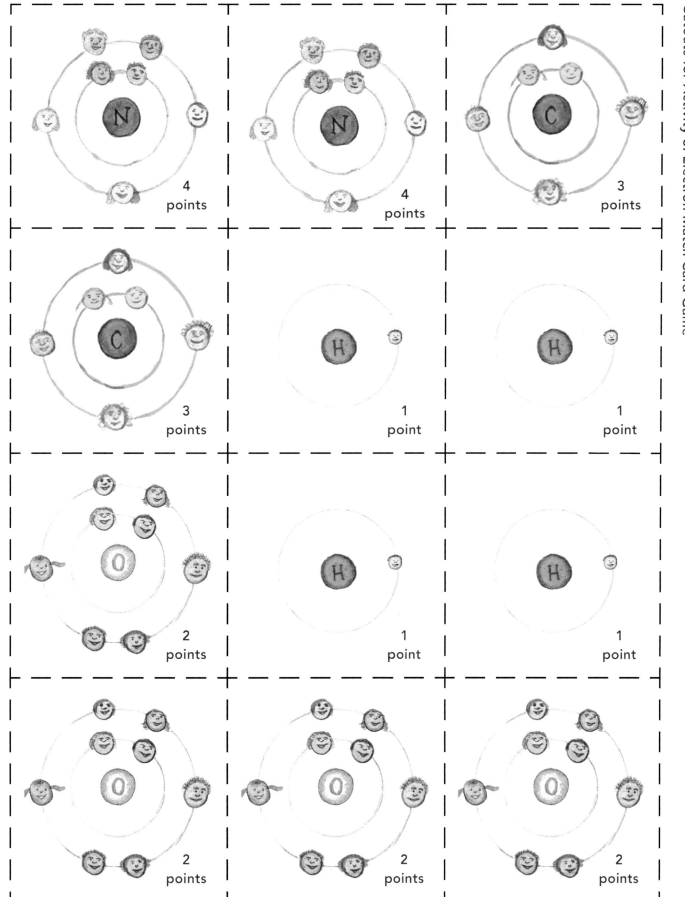

4
points

4
points

3
points

3
points

1
point

1
point

2
points

1
point

1
point

2
points

2
points

2
points

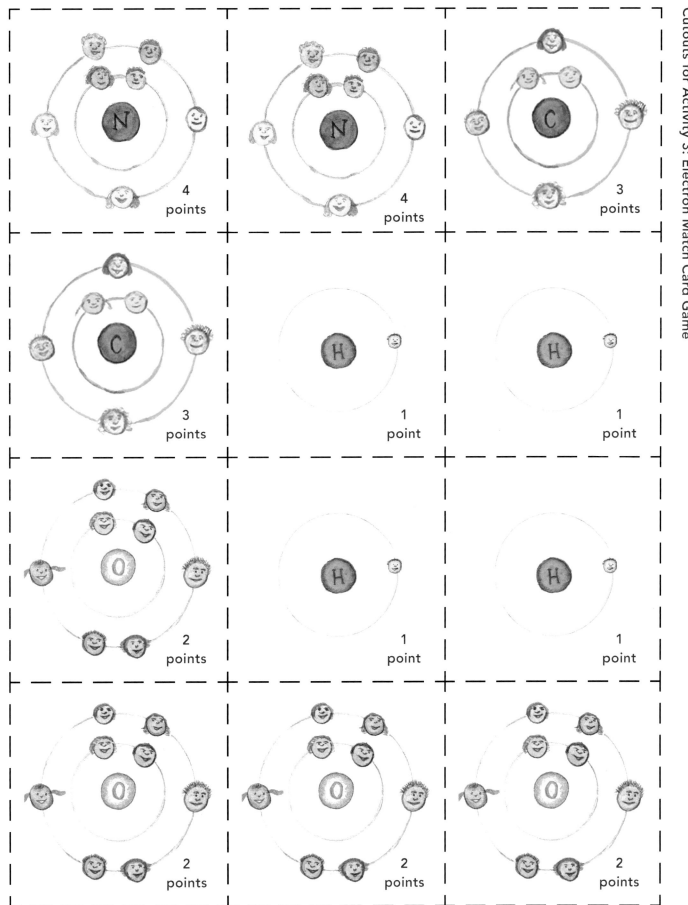

4
points

4
points

3
points

3
points

1
point

1
point

2
points

1
point

1
point

2
points

2
points

2
points

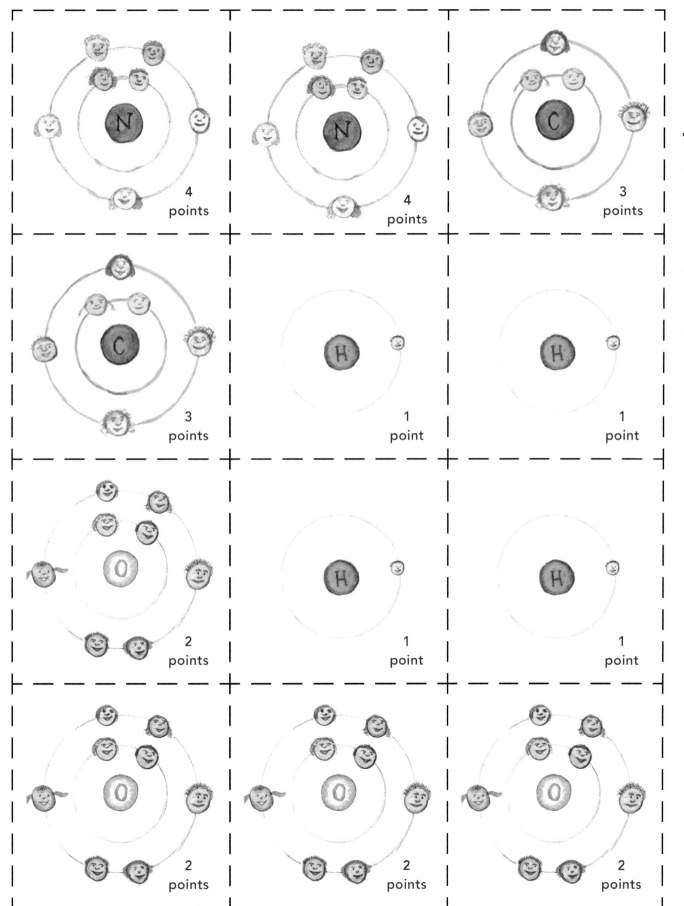

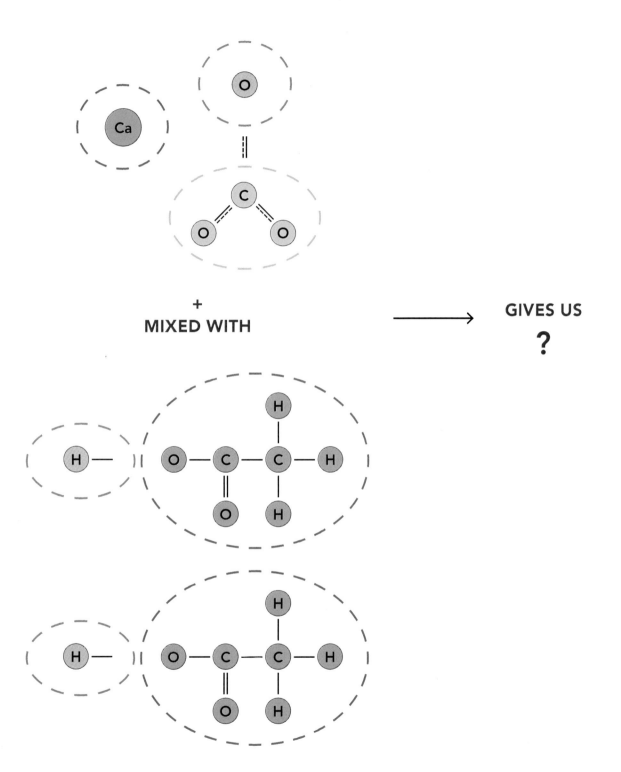

+

MIXED WITH

GIVES US

?

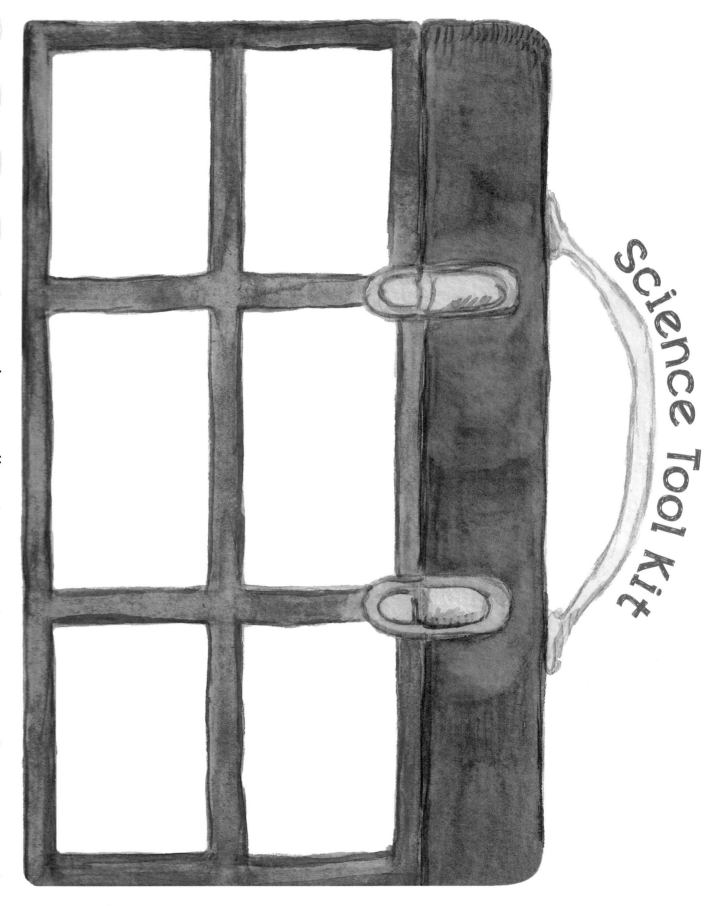

Science Tool Kit

Made in the USA
Middletown, DE
13 October 2016